THE MOST IMPORTANT
WORDS
Jesus EVER SPOKE

THE MOST IMPORTANT WORDS *Jesus* EVER SPOKE

What He Said to His Followers Before Ascending to Heaven

Why They Matter Now—For the End Times

CAPT. DALE BLACK

BLACK EAGLE
PUBLISHING, LLC

ISBN: 978-1-965343-05-0   (Print)

ISBN: 978-1-965343-06-7   (E-book)

10 9 8 7 6 5 4 3 2 1

CONTENTS

WHY THESE WORDS STILL SPEAK TODAY

How to Read This Book

This book is not meant to be rushed.

Each chapter invites you to pause and reflect on the final words of Jesus as recorded through four distinct Gospel witnesses. You may read it straight through, one Gospel at a time, or slowly—one chapter per day—allowing the words to settle into your heart.

As you read:

- Consider **who Jesus is** in each Gospel.
- Notice **what He says, to whom**, and **why**.

- Ask yourself **how these final words speak into your own life** today.

You don't need theological training to understand this book—only a willing heart. Read prayerfully. Reflect honestly. And allow the Holy Spirit to guide you into deeper truth, hope, and faith.

These are not just Jesus's last words.
They are living words—still speaking.

The Weight of Last Words

Throughout history, people have been captivated by last words.

We instinctively pay attention when someone's final moments are spoken. Books are written, documentaries produced, and countless videos created with titles like *The Last Words of Famous Figures* or *What They Said Before They Died.* Whether it's a statesman, a writer, an entertainer, or a historical hero, we believe—often rightly—that final words carry special weight.

Why?

Because last words tend to strip away pretense.
They reveal what remains when time runs out.
They show us what mattered most.

I've always loved history, when it's true. I enjoy learning about the sayings of great thinkers and leaders—men like Mark Twain, Winston Churchill, and Ronald Reagan. Their words often reflected hard-earned wisdom, humor under pressure, courage in crisis, or clarity born from long experience.

But as meaningful as those words may be, none of them compare to the final words spoken by Jesus Christ.

And that realization is what led me to write about the last words of the Lord.

Four Gospels. One Cross. Eternal Words.

The last words of Jesus were not spoken in comfort, safety, or reflection at the end of a long life. They were spoken from and around a Roman cross—amid pain, humiliation, injustice, and unimaginable physical suffering.

Yet what Jesus spoke was not confusion or despair.
It was intention.
It was fulfillment.
It was love.

What makes these words even more remarkable is that they are recorded for us in **four separate Gospel accounts**—the Gospel of Matthew, the Gospel of Mark, the Gospel of Luke, and the Gospel of John.

Each writer tells the same story—but from a different vantage point.

That's not a weakness.
It's a strength.

Just as four eyewitnesses to an event will emphasize different details while describing the same truth, the four Gospels together give us a fuller, richer understanding of Jesus's final moments on earth.

Why the Gospels Don't Sound the Same

One of the first things readers notice is that Jesus's final words are not recorded identically in all four accounts. Some accounts appear in one Gospel and not another. Some emphasize discipleship, others power, others prayer.

This is not contradiction—it is perspective. This is completion.

Matthew writes with the voice of prophecy fulfilled.
Mark writes with urgency toward helping human suffering.
Luke highlights faith through the power of the Holy Spirit.
John reveals divine purpose and completion.

Each Gospel writer was inspired to record **what God wanted most for each audience**, while the Holy Spirit ensured the eternal truths were preserved.

Together, these accounts don't compete—they complement.

More Than History—Words for Living

This series is not about academic debate or theological sparring. It's about learning to *hear His voice.*

I believe the final words of Jesus were not only meant to be remembered—they were meant to be **received**, **pondered**, and **lived**.

They help us navigate

- suffering we don't understand
- forgiveness we struggle to give
- faith when circumstances scream otherwise
- hope when the story seems unfinished

In my own life, I've found that meditating on these words has a way of quieting the noise and refocusing on what truly matters.

That's what I hope this series does for you.

Learning Together, Not Lecturing

I want you to know something important as we begin: I'm learning right alongside you.

This is not a polished lecture from on high. It's a shared journey of reflection—pausing long enough to let the most powerful words ever spoken sink in.

We live in a world flooded with opinions, outrage, and endless commentary. But sometimes the most life-changing thing we can do is slow down and listen again to words we thought we already knew.

Why These Words Still Matter Today

Jesus's final words were spoken nearly two thousand years ago—but they have lost none of their power.

They speak to

- the wounded heart
- the searching mind
- the weary believer
- the questioning soul

They remind us that even in suffering, God is at work.
Even in silence, Heaven is not absent.
Even in death, the story is not over.

Where We're Going Next

In the coming pages, we'll walk through each Gospel account carefully—one at a time—allowing each to speak in its own voice.

We'll look at

- what Jesus said,
- why it mattered then,
- and how it speaks to us now.

Not rushed. Not forced. Just thoughtfully, prayerfully, and honestly.

So, let's begin—together—by listening again to the last words of Jesus.

Because some words don't fade with time.
They echo into eternity.

Final Words That Point Beyond This World

Three voices. Three lives. One eternal horizon.

Before we listen to the final words of Jesus recorded in the Gospels, it is worth pausing to hear a few last words spoken by men whose lives left a lasting imprint on history. These are not Scripture. They do not carry divine authority. Yet they disclose something profoundly human—and deeply revealing.

When life draws to a close, pretense falls away. Achievement fades. What remains is clarity. Final words often reveal where a person placed their hope, their confidence, or their fear as they stepped from time into eternity.

These three brief statements remind us that **last words matter**—and they quietly prepare our hearts to listen more carefully to the words of Jesus Christ.

John Wesley (1703–1791)

Founder of Methodism | Preacher of grace and holiness

Surrounded by friends near the end of his life, John Wesley gathered his remaining strength and spoke these simple words:

"The best of all is, God is with us."

After a lifetime spent preaching faith in Christ, Wesley's final declaration was not about his ministry, his legacy, or his works—but about the abiding presence of God. In his final breath, his confidence rested not in what he had done for God, but in what God had done for him.

Source: Recorded by eyewitnesses present at Wesley's death; documented in Wesleyan biographies and historical records.

D. L. Moody (1837–1899)

Evangelist | Proclaimer of the gospel to millions

As Dwight L. Moody lay dying, those around him thought he was dreaming. Suddenly, he opened his eyes and said,

> ***"Earth recedes; heaven opens before me."***

Moments later, he added,

> ***"This is my triumph; this is***
> ***my coronation day."***

Moody did not speak of death as defeat, but as victory. For him, Heaven was not a distant hope—it was an approaching reality. His final words echo the promise that for the believer, death is not an ending, but an entrance.

Source: Eyewitness accounts from family members and ministry associates; documented in multiple Moody biographies.

Sir Thomas Scott (1747–1821)

British politician and author

Sir Thomas Scott's final words stand in stark contrast. Near the end of his life, he spoke with deep urgency:

> ***"Until this moment, I thought there***
> ***was neither a God nor a hell. Now I***

> *know and feel that there are both—*
> *and I am doomed to perdition."*

These words are sobering. They remind us that clarity often comes too late, and that eternity is not shaped by intention, education, or success—but by truth. Scott's final confession serves as a warning: What we believe about God and Christ in this life matters forever.

Source: Documented by those present at his death and preserved in historical Christian writings.

These human voices—one confident, one triumphant, one tragic—now give way to the words that matter most. The words of Jesus Christ.

A Prayer Before We Begin

Dearest Father in Heaven,
As I open these pages, I pause to honor You.
Quiet my heart and clear my thoughts, that I may truly hear Your message.
Let Your final words—the words of Jesus—speak freshly to me today, bringing light where there is darkness, hope where there is weariness, and belief where there is doubt.
Increase my faith, dear Father.
Teach me through Your Word.
Draw me closer to You.

And let what I read not remain on the page but take root in my heart.
I pray this in Jesus's name.
Amen.

This book could save your life. — **Rhonda McCue,** Hospice Nurse

Doctors gave her 3-6 months to live. Eighteen months after diagnosis, her advanced-stage cancer was gone, without chemotherapy or radiation. That was over twenty-five years ago.

PaulaBlack.org

Chapter One

THE GOSPEL OF MATTHEW

ALL AUTHORITY—AND A LIVING COMMISSION

The final chapter of the **Gospel of Matthew** opens not with calm reflection, but with motion—people running, hearts pounding, emotions colliding.

Some of the women had gone to the tomb with **fear and great joy**. Fear, because everything they thought they knew had been shattered. Joy, because something miraculous had begun to dawn. As they ran to tell the disciples that Jesus had risen, the unthinkable happened:

Jesus met them on the road.

His first word to them was simple, powerful, and full of life:

"**Rejoice!**" — Matthew 28:9

They fell at His feet. They held on to Him. They worshiped Him.
Then Jesus spoke again—not with rebuke, not with urgency, but with reassurance:

"Do not be afraid. Go *and* tell My brethren to go to Galilee, and there they will see Me." — Matthew 28:10

Fear gave way to faith.
Confusion gave way to calling.

Worship . . . and Doubt

Soon after, "the eleven disciples went away into Galilee, to the mountain which Jesus had appointed for them. When they saw Him, they worshiped Him." — Matthew 28:16–17

But Matthew adds an honest detail—one that comforts every sincere believer:

"But some **doubted**." — Matthew 28:17

This is important. Jesus did not wait for perfect faith before speaking. He did not delay His mission until everyone felt strong, confident, or fully convinced.

Instead, **He came closer**.

The Authority Behind the Words

Jesus spoke words that still shape history:

"All authority has been given to Me in heaven and on earth." — Matthew 28:18

This statement cannot be overemphasized.

Jesus did not say *some* authority.
He did not say *future* authority.
He said **all authority**—right now.

He was declaring that

- Heaven recognizes His authority.
- Earth is under His authority.
- History unfolds under His authority.

Everything that follows flows from this one truth: All authority belongs to Him.

A Commission, Not a Commandment of Pressure

Because He has all authority, Jesus then gave instruction—not coercion, not force, not manipulation:

"Go therefore and make disciples of all the nations."
— Matthew 28:19

The word *nations* here does not mean political borders or governments. It means **people groups**—men and women from every background, language, culture, and walk of life.

Jesus was not calling His followers to pressure others. He was instructing them to **invite**.

To go willingly.
To love genuinely.
To share truth graciously.

Disciples are not manufactured—they are **formed**.

Baptized Into a Living Relationship

Jesus continued:

"Baptizing them in the name of the Father and of the Son and of the Holy Spirit." — Matthew 28:19

This is not a ritual of religion—it is a declaration of relationship.

- The **Father**, who loves and sends
- The **Son**, who saves and redeems
- The **Holy Spirit**, who empowers and guides

Jesus had already promised that the Father would send the Holy Spirit to His followers—a promise fulfilled at Pentecost, shortly after His ascension. From that moment forward, believers would never walk alone.

Teaching, Not Controlling

Jesus added:

"Teaching them to observe all things that I have commanded you." — Matthew 28:20

Notice the tone: teaching, not controlling.
Guiding, not dominating.
Truth offered with patience and love.

The goal was never outward compliance—but inward transformation.

The Most Comforting Promise

Then Jesus ended with words that may be the most reassuring of all:

"And lo, I am with you always, *even* to the end of the age." — Matthew 28:20

He did not promise ease.
He did not promise safety.
He promised **presence**.

No matter what happens in the world.
No matter what happens in our own lives.
No matter how dark the hour may become.

He is with us.

Until the End of the Age

Jesus spoke of "the end of the age," a phrase rich with meaning. Many believers understand this as pointing toward the closing of the Church Age and the fulfillment of God's prophetic timetable—including what Scripture refers to as the seventieth week of Daniel.

Whatever way one interprets the timing, the promise remains unshaken:

Jesus will be with His people—to the very end.

Not partially.
Not occasionally.
Not symbolically.

But truly, faithfully, always.

Why Matthew's Ending Matters

Matthew does not end his Gospel with Jesus disappearing into Heaven. He ends with Jesus **sending His followers**

into the world, anchored by authority and sustained by presence.

The final message is clear:

- Jesus reigns.
- Jesus sends.
- Jesus remains.

And because He is still with us, the story is not over.

Looking Ahead

Matthew shows us a risen King with all authority, entrusting His mission to imperfect people—and promising never to leave them.

In the next chapter, we will turn to Mark's Gospel, where the focus shifts from **authority**—to the **signs that follow those who believe.**

The same Jesus.
A different lens.
And more truth waiting to be discovered.

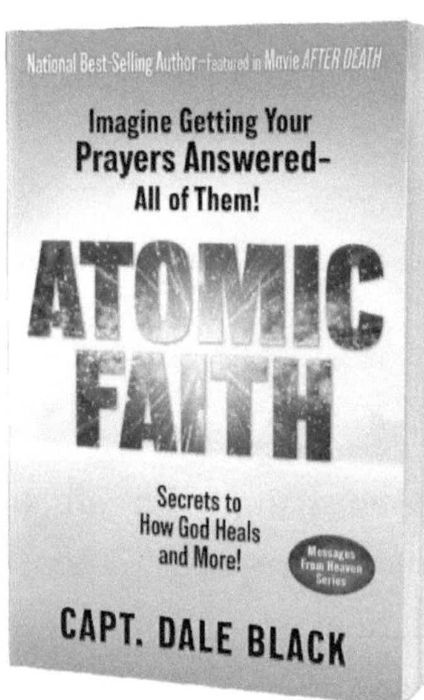

Unlock the Secrets to How God Heals!

If your prayers aren't being answered, the problem isn't you. The raw, powerful truths Jesus taught about faith have been buried under religion, lies, and misinformation.

Atomic Faith is packed with real-life stories of celebrities and ordinary people who tapped into God's power by discovering what faith truly is and how it works.

Discover what can happen when faith goes atomic.

DaleBlack.org

Chapter Two

THE GOSPEL OF MARK

THE GOSPEL CONFIRMED— AND SIGNS THAT FOLLOW THOSE WHO BELIEVE

Mark's ending moves fast—just like the entire **Gospel of Mark**. It's direct. It's intense. And honest about something many believers have felt at one time or another:

Unbelief.

After Jesus "rose early on the first *day* of the week, He appeared first to **Mary Magdalene**"—the same woman from "whom He had cast seven demons. She went and told" the disciples, who were mourning and weeping. — Mark 16:9–10

But when they heard that Jesus was alive and that Mary had seen Him, **"they did not believe."** — Mark 16:11

That detail matters, because it shows us something real: Even people who have walked with Jesus can struggle to believe when life knocks the wind out of them.

Grief can cloud the mind.
Fear can tighten the heart.
Disappointment can silence hope.

And yet . . . Jesus did not give up on them. He expected change. Their unbelief gave way to belief as they witnessed and experienced the truth for themselves.

When Good News Feels Too Good to Be True

Mark tells us Jesus appeared again—this time to two disciples as they walked into the country. They reported it to the others, but again:

"They did not believe them either." — Mark 16:13

This is not just a story about ancient disciples. This is a story about human nature.

Sometimes the Lord is doing something wonderful—right in front of us—but our minds keep replaying what went wrong . . . yesterday.

Sometimes we've been hurt, and we protect ourselves by refusing to believe.

Sometimes we can believe God's promises for "other people" but struggle to believe the same promises for ourselves.

A Loving Rebuke—and a Fresh Start

Later, Jesus appeared to the eleven remaining disciples. And Mark says Jesus **"rebuked their unbelief and hardness of heart**, because they did not believe those who had seen Him after He had risen." — Mark 16:14

That word *rebuked* may sound harsh—until we understand what it really is:

A rebuke from Jesus is not rejection.
It is correction.

I've met many people who struggle with the word *rebuke*.

Jesus wasn't saying, "I'm done with you."
He was saying, "Come back to truth."

And then—beautifully—He didn't just correct them.
He **commissioned** them.

The Message That Saves

Jesus said,

"Go into all the world and preach the gospel to every creature." — Mark 16:15

Mark records the gospel invitation in clear terms:

"He who believes and is baptized will be saved; but he who does not believe will be condemned." — Mark 16:16

This is a key point for us all.

Salvation begins with **inner belief**—a heart-level trust in who Jesus is and what He has done. Baptism is the **outward step** of obedience that openly identifies a person with Christ.

And notice: Jesus puts the spotlight on belief.
Those who refuse Him remain under condemnation—not because God is cruel, but because they **reject** the only cure for sin.

Here's a simple way to say it:

- **Faith in Jesus opens the door to connection with God.**

- **Rejecting Jesus leaves a person right where they already are—separated from God.**

That's not meant to scare people. It's meant to **save** people.

Signs That Follow Faith

Then Jesus spoke words that are both sobering and thrilling:

"And these signs will follow those who believe." — Mark 16:17

In Mark's account, these signs include

- casting out demons in Jesus's name
- speaking with new tongues
- supernatural protection in dangerous situations
- laying hands on the sick and the sick recovering

What Jesus said in the sixteenth chapter of Mark is mind-bogglingly wonderful. And it works. I'm not sharing theory—I'm sharing truth that has been proven in real life. If you're unsure of what I mean, I invite you to explore the testimonies found in these books: *Flight to Heaven*; *Life, Cancer, and God*; and *Atomic Faith* and its companion *Workbook*; as well as *Visiting Heaven*. These are not stories of religion, but of transformation—lived-out faith that confirms the words Jesus spoke.

Now, let's return to Mark's Gospel and look more closely at what Jesus said—and what He expected His followers to believe, receive, and live out.

Mark closes with this powerful summary:

The disciples "went out and preached everywhere, **the Lord working with *them* and confirming the word through accompanying signs.**" — Mark 16:20

Said another way:

The gospel was not just spoken—it was demonstrated.

Not to entertain crowds.
Not to build personalities.
Not to put on a show.

But to confirm one thing:

Jesus is alive. Jesus has authority. And following Jesus results in a life of power and blessings.

A Wise and Important Clarification

One part of this passage mentions taking up serpents and drinking anything deadly without harm. It's important to read that in the spirit of the entire Bible.

This is not permission to test God.
This is not a dare.
This is not a stunt.

It is a picture of God's **protection** when believers face danger in the course of obedience—especially in the early church as the gospel advanced into hostile places.

In plain language:

God protects His people—but we do not tempt Him.

Faith is courageous.
Faith is not reckless.

The Big Lesson of Mark's Ending

Jesus's closing teaches at least three life-changing truths in Mark 16:14–20:

1. Unbelief can show up even in sincere people.

But Jesus is not shocked by it—and He is not finished with us when it appears.

2. The gospel of Jesus laying down His life so that we can be saved is for every person.

Not just the "religious." Not just the "good."
Every creature. Every background. Every story.

3. Jesus still works through His people.

Mark doesn't end with a distant Savior. He ends with a living Lord:

- sending
- working
- confirming
- helping
- saving
- healing
- delivering

That's why this matters to us today.

Remember this too:

***Just as light drives out darkness—
belief drives out unbelief.***

Looking Ahead

Matthew ends with **commission**.
Mark ends with **signs following those who believe**.

And now we turn to Luke—where the lens shifts again.

Luke will show us the heart of Jesus in a deeply personal way:
the promise of the Father—**power from on high**.

Mark describes the signs that follow those who believe.
Luke speaks of the promise of the Father—the spiritual power Heaven releases into the life of the believer.

Let's continue.

Atomic Faith
WORKBOOK

* Over 101 activities to take effective action.

* Chapter summaries with key *takeaways*.

* Faith principles with practical suggestions.

* Easy to follow ideas to get results.

* And MUCH more!

Order at:
DaleBlack.org/Store

Dale Black
DaleBlack.org

When you or someone you love is diagnosed with CANCER... emotions can feel overwhelming. Fear and panic often follow the countless questions that flood your mind. In moments like these, it's natural to search for hope and direction.

Drawing from more than 25 years as a Christian healing coach and cancer survivor, Paula Black shares encouraging, practical and faith-filled insight rooted in the Bible. To learn more and continue your journey of healing, visit:

PaulaBlack.org

THE GOSPEL OF LUKE

OPENS MINDS AND PROMISES POWER AND GREAT JOY

The closing chapter of the **Gospel of Luke** gives us something precious—something every believer was meant to experience, yet in today's society, it is rarely found.

Luke writes about **Jesus opening minds, revealing purpose**, and **promising power**.

Understanding Comes Before Assignment

After His resurrection, Jesus spoke these words to His disciples:

"These *are* the words which I spoke to you while I was still with you, that all things must be fulfilled which were written **in the Law** of Moses **and** *the* Prophets **and** *the* Psalms concerning Me." — Luke 24:44

Then Luke records something remarkable:

"And He opened their understanding, that they might comprehend the Scriptures." — Luke 24:45

This is a quiet but powerful moment.

The disciples had heard Jesus teach for years. They knew the Scriptures. But now, something changed—not in the text but *inside* each of *them*.

Fasten your seatbelt. Wait for it!

Jesus **opened their understanding**!

This reminds us of important truths:

- Knowledge alone is not enough.
- Familiarity is not the same as understanding.
- Scripture requires **Holy Spirit illumination**.

Until the Spirit of God opens our understanding, the Bible can feel confusing, distant, or fragmented. But when the Holy Spirit brings illumination, the pieces all fit.

I warned you to fasten your seatbelt. This is why. When Jesus opens our understanding, He carries us to a higher way of seeing.

The Message at the Center

Jesus then summarized the **heart of the gospel**:

"Thus it is written, and thus it was necessary for the Christ to suffer and to rise from the dead the third day" — Luke 24:46

The suffering was not accidental.
The resurrection was not optional.

Both were **necessary**.

And from that finished work flows the message believers are to carry:

"And that repentance and remission of sins should be preached in His name to all nations." — Luke 24:47

Repentance is a change of heart and direction.
Remission of sins is complete forgiveness.

Together, they form the doorway into new life.

Witnesses—But Not Yet Ready

Jesus told them plainly:

"You are witnesses of these things." — Luke 24:48

They had seen Him suffer.
They had seen Him risen.
They had heard His words.

Yet—even with all of that—Jesus did **not** send them out immediately.

Instead, He gave them a command that might surprise us.

The Promise Before the Mission

Jesus said,

"Behold, I send the **Promise of My Father** upon you; but tarry in the city of Jerusalem until you are **endued with power** from on high." — Luke 24:49

This verse is vital.

Before preaching.
Before traveling.
Before changing the world.

Jesus told His followers to **wait**.

Why?

Because the power of the Holy Spirit would enter them.

Knowledge without spiritual power leads to frustration.
Truth without spiritual power leads to burnout.

Calling without spiritual power leads to struggle.

What they needed—and what we still need—was and is the **power of the Holy Spirit.**

This promise would later be fulfilled in the book of Acts and is often referred to as the **baptism of the Holy Spirit.** But here in Luke, we see how seriously Jesus viewed this moment.

He did not say, "Go and do your best."
He said, "Wait until God empowers you."

**Life as a follower of Jesus was
never meant to be lived apart from
the power of the Holy Spirit.**

God's Power in You

In Luke's Gospel, Jesus did not explain every detail of what this power would look like. That revelation would come later. But He made one thing clear:

**A life following Jesus cannot be
lived successfully without the
power of the Holy Spirit.**

We cannot truly understand Scripture without the Holy Spirit.
We cannot walk in obedience without the Holy Spirit.

We cannot live as Jesus taught us to live without the Holy Spirit.

This truth stands at the heart of the *Messages from Heaven* series, including my book about the Holy Spirit—a reminder that God never intended believers to live the Christian life in their own strength.

Blessed—Then Lifted

Luke then records Jesus's final visible moments with His disciples:

"And He led them out as far as Bethany, and He lifted up His hands and blessed them." — Luke 24:50

Jesus did not leave them with fear.

He left them with a **blessing**.

"Now it came to pass, while He blessed them, that He was parted from them and carried up into heaven." — Luke 24:51

His final posture toward them was not correction or command—it was blessing.

Joy, Worship, and Waiting

The disciples' response is just as striking:

"And they worshiped Him, and returned to Jerusalem with great joy, and were continually in the temple praising and blessing God. Amen." — Luke 24:52–53

Please take a moment and think about that.

Jesus had just left them physically—yet they were filled with **great joy**.

Why?

Because they trusted His **promise**.
Because they believed **help** was coming.
Because they knew they were **not** abandoned.

And so, they waited—not in fear, not in confusion, but in **worship and expectation**—until **endued with power** from on high.

What is missing from most Christians' lives is **power**—the power of the Holy Spirit.

Why Luke's Ending Matters

Luke shows us that before Jesus sends us out, He invites us **in**—into understanding, into promise, and into power.

- Minds opened.
- Hearts anchored.
- Power promised.

Following Jesus was never meant to be lived alone or powerless.

And now, in the final Gospel account, we turn to John—where Jesus speaks not as the Suffering One or the Teacher but as the Son who declares,

"It is finished."

> ****Following Jesus was never meant to be lived in our own strength but with the power of the Holy Spirit.****

Chapter Four

THE GOSPEL OF JOHN

LOVE RESTORED, PURPOSE RENEWED, AND A LIFE THAT FEEDS OTHERS

The final chapter of the **Gospel of John** gives us one of the most personal and tender moments in all of Scripture.

Jesus is no longer suffering.
He is no longer in the tomb.
He is alive—fully risen.

And here, He does something wonderfully ordinary.

He eats breakfast with His disciples. That's fellowship.

This matters. Jesus is not a spirit or an idea. He has risen bodily from the dead. His glorified body is real.

He talks. He eats. He walks with them. The resurrection is not symbolic—it is physical, personal, and powerful.

A Question That Goes Straight to the Heart

After breakfast, Jesus turned His attention to **Simon Peter**.

Peter—the bold one.
Peter—the impulsive one.
Peter—the one who had denied Jesus three times.

Jesus did not accuse him.
Jesus did not shame him.
Jesus asked him a question.

"Simon, *son* of Jonah, do you love Me more than these?"

Peter answered simply and honestly:

"Yes, Lord; You know that I love You."

Jesus responded with purpose:

"Feed My lambs." — John 21:15

Then Jesus asked again:

"Simon, *son* of Jonah, do you love Me?"

Peter answered again:

"Yes, Lord; You know that I love You."

Jesus replied:

"Tend My sheep." — John 21:16

Then Jesus asked a third time:

"Simon, *son* of Jonah, do you love Me?"

This time, Peter was grieved. Not angry—grieved. The question touched the wound of his past failure. Yet Peter answered with humility:

"Lord, You know all things; You know that I love You."

Jesus answered one last time:

"Feed My sheep." — John 21:17

Why Three Times?

Jesus asked Peter three times—not to reopen wounds but to **heal them**.

Peter had denied Jesus three times.
Now Jesus restored him three times.

Every failure was met with grace.
Every denial was met with calling.
Every broken place was met with purpose.

Jesus did not say, "Try harder next time."

He said, "Care for My people."

The Heart of a Shepherd

Jesus used simple language—but it carried deep meaning.

Sheep are not known for strength.
They are not known for brilliance.
They need guidance, protection, and care.

Jesus knows this.

And He entrusts His sheep to people—not because we are perfect shepherds but because we are His hands and feet—called to be the extension of the risen Lord Jesus and empowered by God's Holy Spirit (chapter 3).

A good shepherd

- speaks gently
- leads patiently
- protects fiercely
- corrects lovingly

He does not beat the sheep.
He does not shame them for being slow.
He guides them with care.

Jesus is the Good Shepherd—and He calls His followers to reflect His heart.

Love That Shows Up in Action

Notice what Jesus connected love to.

He did not say, "If you love Me, feel deeply."
He did not say, "If you love Me, speak loudly."

He said,

"If you love Me—feed My sheep."

Love for Jesus is shown through **care for people**.

That care can be simple:

- teaching what Scripture says
- reminding people of God's promises
- encouraging the weary
- pointing others to Jesus, our Savior
- lifting in fervent prayer those God places along our path

You do not need a pulpit.
You do not need a title.
You do not need a platform.

If you love Jesus, you can feed His sheep.

A Glimpse of the Cost—and the Glory

Jesus then spoke quietly about Peter's future:

"When you were younger, you girded yourself and walked where you wished; but when you are old, you will stretch out your hands, and another will gird you and carry *you* where you do not wish." — John 21:18

John explains that Jesus was speaking about the kind of death by which Peter would glorify God.

This is sobering—but also honorable.

Jesus doesn't hide the cost of following Him.
But He also shows us that faithfulness **glorifies God**.

A True Testimony—and an Endless Story

John closes his Gospel with these words:

"This is the disciple who testifies of these things, and wrote these things—and we know that his testimony is true." — John 21:24

Then he adds something breathtaking:

"There are many other things that Jesus did, which if they were written one by one, I suppose that even the world itself could not contain the books that would be written." — John 21:25

In other words:

The story of Jesus is **far greater** than any single book.

And the story of His work did not end when the Gospel accounts ended.

It continues—through His people today.

Why the Gospel of John's Ending Matters

John's Gospel does not end with commands or miracles from Jesus.

He ends with **love**, **restoration**, and **purpose**.

Jesus restored a broken disciple.
Jesus defined what love looks like.
Jesus entrusted ordinary people with extraordinary care.

And He reminds us that the greatest service we can offer Him is this:

Love Him loyally—and feed His sheep.

A Final Word Before We Close the Booklet

You don't have to be perfect.
You don't have to be fearless.
You don't have to have all the answers.

If you love God—love Jesus.
Feed His lambs.
Tend His sheep.

Care for His people.

And as you do, you become part of the story that still cannot be contained.

***Jesus said, "If you love Me—
feed My sheep."***

***Love for Jesus is shown
through care for people.***

Feeding His Sheep from the Quiet Places

When the risen Jesus stood by the Sea of Galilee and spoke to Peter, His words were simple and deeply personal: "Feed My lambs. . . . Tend My sheep. . . . Feed My sheep." — John 21:15–17

Jesus did not explain *how* this feeding must always look. He did not limit it to preaching, traveling, strength, youth, or public ministry. He spoke to the heart of a shepherd—to care, to tend, to nourish what belongs to Him.

That matters more than we often realize.

Many believers reach a season when their physical strength fades, their mobility is limited, or their world becomes very small. Some are confined by illness. Some by age. Some by circumstances beyond their control.

And with that limitation often comes a quiet question: *Do I still matter? Can I still serve?*

The answer from Scripture is a resounding *yes*.

One of the most powerful ways we feed the sheep of Jesus is through **interceding prayer**.

Prayer is not passive. It is not a lesser ministry. It is not something we do only when we can do nothing else. Prayer is active care of the flock.

Samuel understood this when he said,

"Far be it from me that I should sin against the Lord in ceasing to pray for you." — 1 Samuel 12:23

Notice that—**ceasing to pray** was unthinkable to him. He considered lack of prayer for God's people as sin. Intercession was part of his calling, part of his faithfulness, part of how he shepherded God's people.

The apostle Paul lived this same truth. Over and over, he reminded believers that he carried them before God in prayer. Though separated by distance, imprisoned by walls, or limited by circumstances, Paul continued to *feed the churches* by lifting them up to the Lord.

Prayer strengthens the weak.
Prayer guards the vulnerable.
Prayer comforts the weary.

Prayer invites the power of Heaven into places we cannot physically reach.

Recently, I heard from someone whose life had been radically altered by injury—paralyzed from the neck down, unable to serve in any visible way. They felt useless, forgotten, and without purpose. Yet they remembered hearing a simple truth on my YouTube channel: *Even if you can do nothing else, you **can** pray.*

And what a mighty calling that is.

Intercessory prayer is feeding the sheep from the quiet places. It is tending the flock from behind closed doors. It is loving others in partnership with the Great Shepherd Himself.

Jesus never said His sheep would only be fed by strong hands or steady feet. Sometimes they are fed by faithful hearts, whispered prayers, and unseen tears.

If you can pray for others, you are not sidelined in the kingdom of God. You are still doing exactly what Jesus asked.

You are feeding His sheep.

> **When you lift others before the Lord in prayer, you are doing holy work—tending hearts and feeding the sheep Jesus loves.**

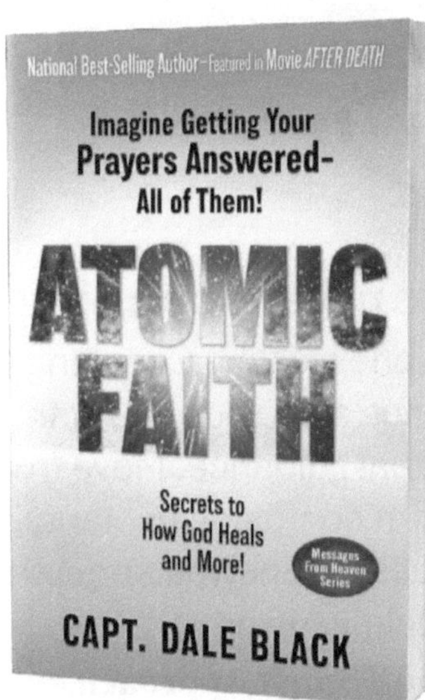

Unlock the Secrets to How God Heals!

If your prayers aren't being answered, the problem isn't you. The raw, powerful truths Jesus taught about faith have been buried under religion, lies, and misinformation.

Atomic Faith is packed with real-life stories of celebrities and ordinary people who tapped into God's power by discovering what faith truly is and how it works.

Discover what can happen when faith goes atomic.

DaleBlack.org

Christian Cancer Coaching

Through one-on-one Healing Coaching, Paula Black comes alongside you with practical and spiritual guidance. Move from fear to peace, from confusion to clarity, and from weakness to renewed strength and healing, using **a**

Body, Soul, and Spirit Approach

"After being diagnosed with stage 4 brain and lung cancer, doctors told me there was nothing more they could do. Then I found Paula's Christian Cancer Coaching. Within just a few months of her coaching and guidance, my strength returned – and today I'm completely cancer-free." – Tommy

PaulaBlack.org

FINAL REFLECTION
FOUR GOSPELS. ONE CROSS. ETERNAL HOPE.

How to Finish Well

When we step back and look at the final words of **Jesus Christ**, one truth becomes clear:

"For God did not send His Son into the world to condemn the world, but that the world through Him might be saved." — John 3:17

Jesus did not simply finish His life. **He finished His mission.**

And in doing so, He showed us how to live—and how to finish—well.

Four Voices. One Message.

Each Gospel gives us a different view of Jesus's final words, yet together they form a single, powerful message.

- **Matthew** shows us **authority** and **commission**—Jesus sends, Jesus gives authority to each believer, and Jesus remains with us to the end.

- **Mark** confronts **unbelief** and reminds us that the gospel is **confirmed by signs** following faithful believers.

- **Luke** opens our understanding and points us to God's promise of the **Holy Spirit—power from on high** that can change the world.

- **John** portrays Jesus **restoring a fallen disciple** and teaching us that following Him involves **loving others** and leading them into a **restored relationship with God** through Jesus.

Different voices.
One Savior.
One unchanging heart of God.

Finishing Well Is Not About Perfection

One of the most encouraging truths in these final moments is this:

Jesus entrusted His authority, His power, and His mission to imperfect people.

Some doubted.
Some feared.
Some had failed badly.

Yet Jesus did not withdraw His calling.

He corrected unbelief.
He restored the fallen.
He **empowered** the weak.
He stayed present with them all.

Finishing well does not mean never stumbling.

It means turning back to God when needed, rising up again in His power, and stepping into your rightful place in His family.

Authority, Power, and Presence

Jesus did not leave His followers empty-handed.

He gave them everything they needed:

- **Authority** – "All authority has been given to Me." — Matthew 28:18

- **Power** – "You [shall be] endued with power from on high." — Luke 24:49

- **Presence** – "I am with you always." — Matthew 28:20

This is the foundation of a life that finishes well.

We are not sent out alone. He is always with us.
We are not expected to live by willpower.
But by His power.
We are not abandoned when the road gets hard.
He will never leave or forsake us.

Love Is the Measure

At the very end, Jesus reduced everything to one simple test:

Do you love Me?

And He defined what love looks like:

Feed My lambs.
Tend My sheep.
Care for My people.

Finishing well is not measured by applause, titles, or recognition.

It is measured by **faithfulness**:

- faithful to follow Jesus,
- faithful to God's Word,
- faithful to the power placed inside us,

often in quiet, unseen ways.

A Life That Points Forward

Jesus's final words were not an ending—they were a beginning.

Because He finished His work,
we can begin ours.

Because He conquered death,
we can live with hope for Heaven.

Because He remains with us,
we can keep going—with the power of the Holy Spirit.

A Gentle Invitation

Wherever you are in your journey—strong or struggling,
confident or uncertain—these words are still for you.

Finish your race by following Jesus.
Finish your days with God's love in your heart.
Finish your calling with power from the Holy Spirit.

And remember:

You don't finish well by being perfect.
You finish well by **staying close to Jesus** . . .
and never quitting.

He finished His work—
so we could walk faithfully in ours.

Closing Blessing

A closing prayer, from me for you:

May the words you have read take deep root in your heart, and may the cross of Jesus come alive with clear and powerful meaning in your life.

I pray that God's Spirit would draw near to you as you draw near to Him and that His Word would become clear, steady, and sure—lighting your path and guiding each step forward.

May the light of the Lord shine upon you, illuminating your way as you move ahead with faith and confidence.

I pray that God would shine His mercy upon you— that He would guide you, direct you, protect you, and richly bless you.

I pray for a long life filled with purpose, strength, health, and blessing, that you may remain firmly planted in the center of God's perfect will.

I pray this in the name of Jesus.

Amen.

ABOUT THE AUTHOR

Capt. Dale Black is an author, minister, missionary, former airline pilot, flight instructor, and aviation business owner whose life was profoundly changed after surviving a devastating plane crash. That experience marked the beginning of a deep personal journey into learning the Bible and a lifelong commitment to understanding and living by faith.

Over the course of his aviation career, Dale trained thousands of pilots as an instructor and check airman. He flew and managed aircraft for celebrities, CEOs, and aviators from all walks of life. His background in aviation shaped both his discipline and his teaching style—clear, practical, and grounded in real-world experience.

Following his recovery from a fatal airplane crash, Dale went on to launch a global ministry, traveling to more than sixty countries to share the gospel of Jesus Christ and to deliver Bibles, food, clothing, and medical supplies to those in need. His work has consistently focused on encouraging believers and seekers alike to trust God in the midst of life's challenges.

Dale continues to write faith-filled books and teach biblical principles that help readers grow in confidence, faith, and perseverance. He is the author of the *Messages from Heaven* book series and shares weekly encouragement through his writing and online ministry.

Learn more at **DaleBlack.org**.

The arrow points to the top of the one-hundred-foot-high memorial to dead aviators, where the plane struck after takeoff from Hollywood-Burbank airport. Two men were killed. A third pilot, Dale Black, was in critical condition and in a coma for three days. Full story recorded in the book *Flight To Heaven*.

Photo taken thirty minutes after the crash. Two firefighters examine the wreckage near one of the aircraft's engines at the base of the Portal of the Folded Wings mausoleum.

Dale Black's aviation memorial plaque was installed in the Portal of the Folded Wings on the fiftieth anniversary of the crash.

Before You Go...

A FREE GIFT FOR You

Beautiful Scripture Promises
to Uplift Your Faith

Don't miss this blessing.

DOWNLOAD YOURS FREE ▶

www.DaleBlack.org/   * Click on Free Downloads

Get God's Word for your heart today.

When you or someone you love is diagnosed with CANCER... emotions can feel overwhelming. Fear and panic often follow the countless questions that flood your mind. In moments like these, it's natural to search for hope and direction.

Drawing from more than 25 years as a Christian healing coach and cancer survivor, Paula Black shares encouraging, practical and faith-filled insight rooted in the Bible. To learn more and continue your journey of healing, visit:

PaulaBlack.org

Christian Cancer Coaching

Through one-on-one Healing Coaching, Paula Black comes alongside you with practical and spiritual guidance. Move from fear to peace, from confusion to clarity, and from weakness to renewed strength and healing, using **a**

Body, Soul, and Spirit Approach

"After being diagnosed with stage 4 brain and lung cancer, doctors told me there was nothing more they could do. Then I found Paula's Christian Cancer Coaching. Within just a few months of her coaching and guidance, my strength returned – and today I'm completely cancer-free." – Tommy

PaulaBlack.org

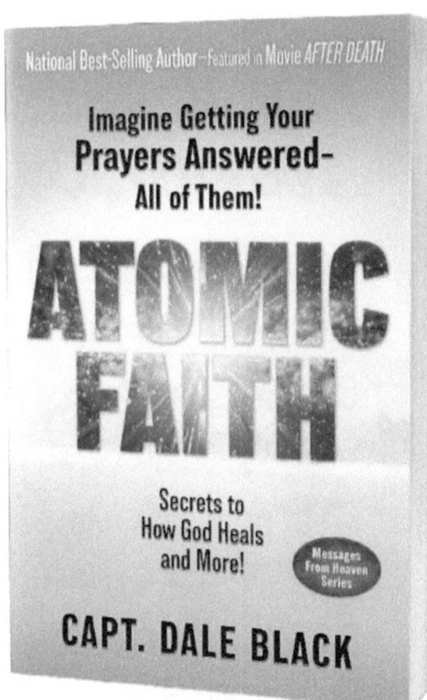

Unlock the Secrets to How God Heals!

If your prayers aren't being answered, the problem isn't you. The raw, powerful truths Jesus taught about faith have been buried under religion, lies, and misinformation.

Atomic Faith is packed with real-life stories of celebrities and ordinary people who tapped into God's power by discovering what faith truly is and how it works.

Discover what can happen when faith goes atomic.

DaleBlack.org

How I Beat Cancer!

This book could save your life. — **Rhonda McCue,** Hospice Nurse

Doctors gave her 3-6 months to live. Eighteen months after diagnosis, her advanced-stage cancer was gone, without chemotherapy or radiation. That was over twenty-five years ago.

PaulaBlack.org

HEAVENLY KEYS
to a life without limits

When Capt. Dale Black survived a horrific plane crash, he awoke from a 3-day coma… changed.

He doesn't try to convince anyone of what happened. He simply shares what he **believes** has forever turned his life upside down.

For those who long for hope beyond this life…

One man's true-from-the-heart story.

DaleBlack.org

Will I go to Heaven?

Many of us quietly wonder what comes after this life. If you'd like to explore what the Bible says about how to get to Heaven — I've created a simple page that shares the good news of Jesus.

Visit: **Book Your Heaven Flight** page to learn more. No pressure. Explore at your own pace.

DaleBlack.org

Scroll down. Bottom of page:
Book Your Heaven Flight

Follow Dale Black

DaleBlack.org

Capt. Dale Black - YouTube

Follow Paula Black

PaulaBlack.org

Paula Black – You Tube

MASTER LIFE COACHING
Faith-based personal & professional guidance
— 1-on-1 with Capt. Dale Black —
DaleBlack.org
Private * Discreet * Limited Availability

www.ingramcontent.com/pod-product-compliance
Lightning Source LLC
Chambersburg PA
CBHW021341060726
47591CB00006B/2125